THE CUISINE OF THE KINGS

On the rich panorama of French regional cuisine, the foods from the Loire Valley are probably less famous (at least in other countries) than those from Normandy, Burgundy, Alsace and the Périgord. However, the menu is as varied, tasty, wholesome and enchanting as all the rest. It offers a true feast for the palate, rich in surprises and...temptations. Lavish recipes recall the opulent tables laid for the Kings of France five hundred years ago in the magnificent castles are still mirrored the calm waters of the Loire. The cuisine, like the architecture between Anjou and Maine, Touraine and Orléans, Sologne, Berry and the surroundings – without neglecting the Pays Nantais with its picturesque estuary – is monumental in its own way. It is hard to find "poor" or "fast" dishes. Here food is not meant for dieters. But, it does offer unforgettable experiences for those who are able to appreciate them with the knowledge that the game is indeed worth the candle. Loire Valley cuisine is strongly tied to a tradition that it lovingly respects, recovers and regenerates and hence it is just as closely tied to the regional products. Excellent fish plays a leading role with an outstanding supporting cast of fresh garden vegetables and fruits, delicious cheeses, fine quality fresh and processed meats, and tasty game from a land that generates superb wines that are used in the kitchen and to accompany the local dishes. Our journey through the cuisine of the Loire region will give you the full picture. Bon voyage and Bon appétit.

THE NUTRITIONIST'S OPINION

Butter, lard, bacon, cream, crème fraîche, and eggs are the tasty but rich ingredients found in northern European cooking and in the foods from the Loire Valley. French cuisine is very colorful and has a definite Mediterranean imprint, as in the Midi for example that differs from the Northern regions' recipes presented here. Not tasting the foods during a marvelous trip between one castle and another would be like betraying the concept of "real" tourism that requires a willingness to sample the culture and foods of other lands. But a trip along the Loire can last a few weeks... then it is best to go back to the Mediterranean diet. The problem would be with loading yourself with so many saturated, animal fats for a whole life. Animal fats of this type transit through the intestines quickly to reach the liver, that faces the major workload because the breakdown of the long carbon chains requires time and energy. Few of the fats are burned immediately, many go into the reserves, or become cholesterol that will remain in the bloodstream for a long time, clogging the arteries. From the health standpoint there is no problem in yielding to temptation during a vacation...after all a vacation is not a lifetime.

"Beurre Blanc" from Nantes ▶

🍲⏱20' ⏲45' 6️⃣ ★

250 gr/$^1/_2$ lb butter
6-7 shallots (about 100 gr/4 oz)
2.5 dl/1 cup white wine vinegar
salt and freshly ground pepper

Kcal 400 P 1 F 35 ⚖

2 Place the saucepan into a larger pan filled with hot water to create a double boiler. Add the butter in pats, melt it slowly and beat with a whisk until the mixture becomes creamy.

The secret behind this sauce is the steady heat and slow cooking in a double-boiler. This sauce is excellent with fish, from trout to salmon and mainly with delicate pike, as described in the next recipe which is a famous dish from the pays Nantais.

1 Clean the shallots and chop them finely. Place them in a small saucepan with the vinegar and slowly bring to a boil; simmer over a low flame until the vinegar is reduced to one quarter of the original amount.

Pike in "Beurre Blanc" ▶

Cut and rinse the pike; but do not remove the scales.
To prepare this dish you need a nice pike (about 1.8 kg/4 lbs to serve 6). Clean the onion, a small leak and a carrot; slice the onion and leak, and cut the carrot into cubes. Place them in a saucepan with 1 liter/1 quart of dry white wine, the thyme, clove, bay leaf, peppercorns and a pinch of coarse salt. Slowly bring to a boil, lower the flame, cover and simmer for 20 minutes.
Let the broth cool and pour it into an appropriately sized fish-kettle, and place the cleaned pike in it.

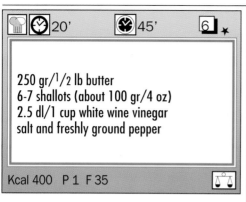

Cover and boil slowly for 20 minutes. Drain the fish, remove the skin and serve it with the *beurre blanc* – a true delight.

🍲⏱20' ⏲30' 4️⃣ ★★

1 pike, approximately 1.8 kg/4 lbs
1 onion
1 carrot
1 leek
1 l/1 quart dry white wine
1 sprig of thyme
1 clove
1 bay leaf
coarse salt
5-6 peppercorns

Kcal 325 P 49 F 2 ⚖

Scallops au Gratin

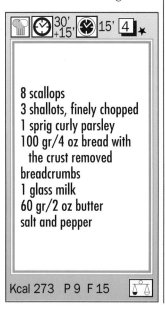

8 scallops
3 shallots, finely chopped
1 sprig curly parsley
100 gr/4 oz bread with the crust removed
breadcrumbs
1 glass milk
60 gr/2 oz butter
salt and pepper

Kcal 273 P 9 F 15

S oak the bread in the milk for 15 minutes before you start. Clean the scallop shells under running water with a brush, open them and remove the flesh. Set 4 shells aside, and if possible, try not to separate the halves.

Rinse the scallops under running water to eliminate any sand and the black part; carefully wash the white part, the orange or "coral" and the hazel colored fringe. Squeeze the fringe to eliminate all water and then chop finely.

Peel and wash the shallots, then chop them finely. Sauté gently in 30 g/1 oz melted butter in a skillet, add the squeezed out bread, the chopped fringe, salt and pepper and stir. Cook for 3-4 minutes and remove from the stove and cool to lukewarm. Distribute the mixture in the 4 shells that you had set aside, and top with the white part, cut in half horizontally, put the "coral" in the middle and cover with the rest of the mixture. Sprinkle lightly with breadcrumbs, put a pat of butter on each and bake at 200 °C/ 390 °F for 15 minutes. Serve immediately.

Potato Torte

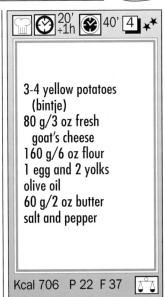

Boil the potatoes in lightly salted water, drain and peel while still hot. Mash the potatoes together with the cheese, butter and egg yolks, add salt and pepper to taste. Blend in the flour and mix with your hands or the mixer until it is smooth without lumps. Shape the dough into a ball and cover with a clean cloth and set aside to rest for 1 hour.

Roll out the dough to a thickness of 1 cm (1/2 inch). Place it in a round baking pan, brush the surface with beaten egg and bake at 180 °C /350 °F for 30 minutes.
Serve immediately.

20' +1h   40'   4   ×★

3-4 yellow potatoes (bintje)
80 g/3 oz fresh goat's cheese
160 g/6 oz flour
1 egg and 2 yolks
olive oil
60 g/2 oz butter
salt and pepper

Kcal 706   P 22   F 37

Asparagus Omelet

| 🧑‍🍳⏰ 10' | ❄️ 15' | 6 ★★ | Kcal 353 P 17 F 29 | ⚖️ |

| 2 dozen small, tender green asparagus | 6 eggs
butter | salt and pepper |

1 Cut off the hard ends of the asparagus, tie them into a bunch and place in a tall, narrow pot – so they stand on end – filled with enough slightly salted water to cover the white part entirely. Cover and bring to a boil, cook for 5-6 minutes and drain. Cut off the white stems, and cut the tips into 3 cm (1 inch) long pieces. Put the asparagus into a frying pan with 3-4 tablespoons butter and cook gently for 3-4 minutes.

2 Beat the eggs with a pinch of salt and pepper, add them to the asparagus, raise the flame so that the eggs begin to set; while the top side is still moist, slide the omelet onto the serving platter, fold it over and serve immediately.

The dining room in the Château de Brissac.

Pork Quiche

🍲🕐 30'+2h 🕐 30' 4 ★★ Kcal 1067 P 22 F 83 ⚖

For the dough:	150 gr/6 oz *Rillettes* (see p. 10)	1 sprig parsley
250 gr/¹/₂ lb flour (plus some more for your work table)	150 gr/6 oz *Rillons* (see p. 37)	1 sprig chives
	1 glass milk	nutmeg
125 gr/5 oz butter, softened	2 dl/³/₄ cup crème fraîche	20 gr/1 tbs butter
1 egg, salt	3 eggs	salt and pepper

1 First prepare the dough. Put the flour in a large bowl, make a well in the middle. Cut the softened butter into pats and put in the middle of the well, add the egg and salt. Beat with an electric mixer, adding a little water as needed until the dough is smooth and free of lumps. It will be ready when it separates from the sides of the bowl.

3 Roll out the dough and line the bottom and edges of a buttered 25 cm (9 inch) baking pan. Evenly arrange the *rillettes* and the *rillons* – breaking them if you have to – on the dough.

2 Shape the dough into a ball, wrap it in a clean cloth and set it aside to rest in a cool place for about 2 hours.

4 Beat the eggs together with the milk and cream; salt and pepper and then add the finely chopped parsley and chives and a pinch of ground nutmeg. Distribute the mixture over the dough, making sure to cover the *rillettes* and *rillons*.
Bake at 220 °C/425 °F for 30 minutes, until the top is evenly browned.

"Rillettes" from Tours

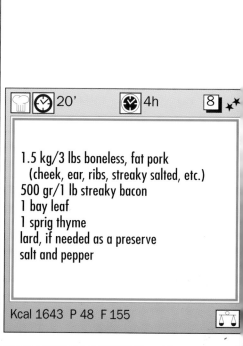

Cut the meats and streaky bacon into chunks, place in a large saucepan (cast iron is best) with 2 liters/2 quarts of water, salt, pepper and the herbs. Cover and bring to the boil slowly, then simmer for at least 4 hours adding a ladle or two of hot water only if necessary, because the meat has to be reduced to a pulp. Remove the herbs and squash the meat with a fork: mix with the grease that formed on the bottom of the saucepan. Place the mixed meats into glass jars with the fat, press down so that the fat comes to the top to form a protective layer to preserve the *rillettes*. You can store it in the refrigerator for a few weeks. If the layer of fat is insufficient, or gets used up, you can add a light layer of pure lard. Serve the *rillettes* at room temperature, spread on country bread – better if it is toasted.

20'   4h   8

1.5 kg/3 lbs boneless, fat pork
(cheek, ear, ribs, streaky salted, etc.)
500 gr/1 lb streaky bacon
1 bay leaf
1 sprig thyme
lard, if needed as a preserve
salt and pepper

Kcal 1643 P 48 F 155

Goat Cheese Quiche

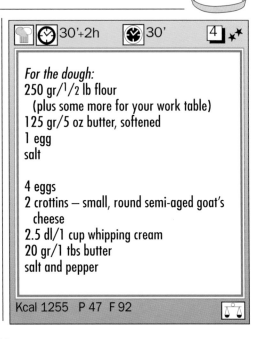

P repare the dough according to the instructions on page 8 (steps 1 and 2). Roll it out and line the bottom and sides of a buttered 25 cm (9 inch) baking pan. Beat the eggs together with the cream and a pinch of salt and pepper, soften the cheese with a fork and add to the mixture. Spread the mixture over the dough and bake at 200 °C/390 °F for 30 minutes.

👨‍🍳 ⏱ 30'+2h ❄ 30' 4 ★★

For the dough:
250 gr/$^1/_2$ lb flour
   (plus some more for your work table)
125 gr/5 oz butter, softened
1 egg
salt

4 eggs
2 crottins – small, round semi-aged goat's
   cheese
2.5 dl/1 cup whipping cream
20 gr/1 tbs butter
salt and pepper

Kcal 1255   P 47   F 92

Asparagus Soup

Wash the asparagus and cut off the tough ends. Tie them into a bunch and place upright in a pot with enough lightly salted water to cover the white part. Cover and simmer for about 20 minutes. Drain; put the cooking water through a strainer and set aside. Cut off the tips and set them aside to decorate the finished soup, and cut the rest of the stems into chunks, discarding the white portion.

Melt the butter in a saucepan and gradually add the flour, stirring constantly until it is golden and there are no lumps.

Add 1 liter/1 quart of the cooking water and the milk. Add the cut stems. Cook

🕐 30' ⏱ 45' 4 ★

800 gr/1 ³/₄ lbs asparagus (preferably giant sized)
1 egg yolk
¹/₂ glass crème fraîche
1 bunch chervil, for garnish
1 glass milk
30 gr/1 oz flour
30 gr/1 oz butter
salt and pepper

Kcal 243 P 8 F 17

slowly for 10 minutes, then remove the asparagus and put through the blender. Put the pureed asparagus

back into the saucepan and heat slowly over a low flame. In the meantime, beat the egg yolk, blend in the crème fraîche and then add to the soup, mixing well to blend. Add the asparagus tips, and salt and pepper to taste. Put the soup into individual bowls and garnish with chopped chervil.

Rabbit Soup

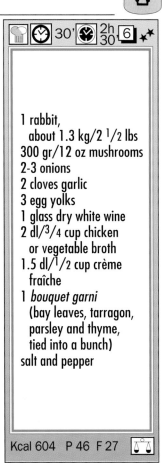

🍳 ⏱ 30' ❄ 2h 30' 6 ✦✦

1 rabbit,
  about 1.3 kg/2 ¹/₂ lbs
300 gr/12 oz mushrooms
2-3 onions
2 cloves garlic
3 egg yolks
1 glass dry white wine
2 dl/³/₄ cup chicken
  or vegetable broth
1.5 dl/¹/₂ cup crème
  fraîche
1 *bouquet garni*
  (bay leaves, tarragon,
  parsley and thyme,
  tied into a bunch)
salt and pepper

Kcal 604   P 46   F 27

Cut the cleaned and gutted rabbit into 10-12 pieces, taking care not to splinter the bones. Put it in a large saucepan with the cut onions, chopped garlic, the *bouquet garni*, a glass of wine and the broth. Cover and bring to the boil, skimming frequently. Once it reaches the boil, lower the flame to the minimum and simmer for about 2 hours until the meat separates readily from the bones. Put the rabbit and the contents of the pan through a fine strainer, pouring the cooking liquid into another saucepan. Discard the *bouquet garni* and carefully bone the rabbit; discard the bones. Put the meat through the blender at low speed until it is a smooth puree.
Clean the mushrooms, dis-card the stems and add to the rabbit purée; set 2-3 tablespoons of mushrooms aside for garnish. Slowly bring the strained cooking liquid to the boil and add the pureed rabbit meat and mushrooms. Salt and pepper to taste and simmer for 15 minutes over a very low flame. In the meantime, beat the yolks together with the crème fraîche, adding the mushrooms you had set aside and one cup of the hot soup. Pour the contents of the mixing bowl into the saucepan with the soup, stir gently to blend, and heat slowly taking care not to let it boil. Serve immediately, with a few sprigs of tarragon for garnish.

Vegetable Soup with Bacon

1 Scald the bacon in hot water; drain, rinse in cold water and dry. Trim the hide and any tough parts; cut it into oblique strips (lardons). Clean the cabbage, discard the tough outer leaves and the core, and cut it into quarters. Separate the leaves and dip them into water containing $1/2$ glass of vinegar; drain and then scald in lightly salted boiling water. Drain well and set aside.

3 Add the cabbage, bacon and chicken broth. Cover, and bring to the boil over a medium flame. Lower the flame to the minimum and simmer for about 1 hour.

4 Salt and pepper to taste; 7-8 minutes before the cooking time has elapsed add the peas, stir and remove the saucepan from the stove. Place the toasted bread in individual bowls; pour the hot soup over the bread and serve immediately.

2 Clean the leeks and onions, cutting off the entire green stem and cut into disks. Peel the turnips and cut into cubes. Put the turnips, onions and leeks into a saucepan: cover and cook for 10 minutes in the melted butter.

1 small savoy cabbage	250 gr/^{1}/$_2$ lb small turnips	^{1}/$_2$ glass of white wine vinegar
350 gr/13 oz streaky bacon	300 gr/12 oz shelled peas	40 g/2 tbs butter
(not smoked)	(frozen is fine)	salt and pepper
8 green onions	toasted bread slices	
300 gr/12 oz leeks	1.5 l/1.5 qts chicken broth	

1 domestic duck, 2 kg/4 1/2 lbs, with the liver 6 tomatoes 4 onions 60 gr/2 oz butter	*For the stuffing:* 1 egg 1 onion 2-3 slices of stale bread, without the crust	1 shallot 1 sprig thyme 1 sprig rosemary 1 dl/3/8 cup milk salt and pepper

Roast Duck with Vegetables

1 Crumble the bread and soak it in the milk for 15 minutes; squeeze it out and put it in a bowl. Finely chop the onion, shallot and duck liver and combine with the bread. Add the thyme and rosemary, salt and pepper and a beaten egg.

3 Slice the onions, cut the tomatoes into chunks, removing the seeds. Put the duck into a large enough baking dish and surround it with the sliced onions and tomatoes, sprinkle with melted butter, add salt and pepper; bake at 200 °C/390 °F for one and a half hours.

2 Stuff the duck with the mixture, close with the cavity with cooking thread; cover with a clean cloth and refrigerate over night.

4 When the duck is done, open it, remove the stuffing and place it in a saucepan. Put the cooking residues with the onions and tomatoes through the blender and then add it to the stuffing. Bring to a boil over a medium blame, lower the flame and reduce the mixture for 5 minutes stirring constantly. Salt and pepper to taste. Slice the duck and serve with the sauce in a gravy boat.

Roast Duck in Muscadet

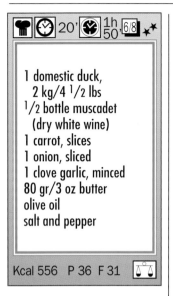

🍴 ⏱ 20' 🕐 1h 50' 6/8 ★✦

1 domestic duck,
2 kg/4 ¹/₂ lbs
¹/₂ bottle muscadet
(dry white wine)
1 carrot, slices
1 onion, sliced
1 clove garlic, minced
80 gr/3 oz butter
olive oil
salt and pepper

Kcal 556 P 36 F 31

S alt and pepper the duck inside and out; remove the neck and wings and cut into pieces.
Put the pieces in a large, warm oven dish; brush the duck with 30 gr/1 oz butter and 1 tablespoon olive oil, and place it on top of the small pieces. The duck should be on its side, resting on a leg.
Bake at 240 °C/460 °F for about 30 minutes. Turn it over onto the other leg and bake for another half hour. Remove the dish from the oven, turn the duck onto its back and bake for 45 minutes, basting frequently with its own juices. While it is baking clean and slice the onion and carrot, chop the garlic finely.
Remove from the oven and keep the duck warm. Eliminate nearly all the cooking grease from the bottom of the pan, add the onion, carrot and garlic, and sauté over a medium flame; pour one glass of water and all the wine over it; lower the flame and gradually reduce the liquid by two thirds. In the meantime, melt the remaining butter in a small saucepan and cook until it is a hazelnut brown (*beurre noisette*); strain the sauce through a fine sieve and add the *beurre noisette*, pour into a gravy boat and serve with the duck.

The Château de Gien mirrored in the Loire River.

Young Wild Boar Stew

1 Wash and peel the vegetables for the marinade. Cut the meat into chunks and place in a bowl with the wine, 5-6 peppercorns, the sliced carrot and onion, the shallot and crushed clove of garlic, and the *bouquet garni*. Marinate for 8 hours turning the meat every now and then.

3 Pour the marinade and enough hot water to cover over the meat. Bring to the boil again; in the meantime, place the vegetables from the marinade into a cheesecloth bag. When the marinade boils add the bag, cover the saucepan, lower the flame to the minimum and simmer for 2 hours, stirring every now and then.

2 Cut the bacon into strips and put into a saucepan filled with cold water; bring to the boil and cook for 5-6 minutes.
Put the meat chunks and the solid parts of the marinade through a strainer and put the vegetables aside; keep the liquid as well. Drain the meat, and brown it slowly in a tablespoon of melted lard. Add the drained bacon strips and a sprinkling of flour and cook quickly over a high flame, stirring.

4 Wash and peel the mushrooms, and sauté in a small skillet with half the butter. Clean the onions and sauté in a saucepan with the rest of the butter and 2-3 tablespoon water; when the water has evaporated add the sugar, stir gently and continue cooking until golden. When the onions are done, place the meat onto a hot serving platter, squeeze the cheesecloth bag over the saucepan to extract the juices; remove from the stove. Combine the pig's blood with a tablespoon of vinegar and blend into the cooking residues. Cover the wild boar chunks with this sauce and serve with the pearl onions and mushrooms.

For the marinade:
1 carrot
1 onion
1 shallot
1 clove garlic
1 *bouquet garni* (bay leaf, tarragon, parsley and thyme, tied together)

black peppercorns
$^1/_2$ l/2 cups red wine

800-900 gr/2 lbs young wild boar meat (preferably shoulder)
150 gr/6 oz mildly salted streaky bacon

10-12 pearl onions
100 gr/4 oz mushrooms
3-4 tablespoon pig blood
1 tablespoon flour
1 tablespoon wine vinegar
1 teaspoon sugar
lard, 40 gr/2 oz butter
salt and pepper

1.5 kg/3 lbs veal (rump or fillet end of the leg) 200 gr/8 oz pork rind 3 onions	6 carrots 3 dl/1 $^1/_4$ cups dry white wine 1 small glass of eau de vie/marc	$^1/_2$ l/2 cups beef broth 1 bouquet of bay leaves and thyme tied together 2 dl/$^3/_4$ cup crème fraîche

Roast Veal with Vegetables

1 Wash and peel the onions and carrots. Make sure that there are no bristles on the pork rind, if necessary singe it, and then rinse under cold running water. Cut it into strips and place, fat side down, on the bottom of an oven pan that has a lid. Cover with alternating layers of carrot circles and sliced onion.

3 Remove the baking pan from the oven, and pour on the wine, a small glass of water and the broth. Add the bouquet, salt and pepper, cover the pan and put it back into the oven for 1 hour; then lower the oven temperature to 150 °C/300 °F and bake for one more hour.

2 Place the veal (tied if necessary) on top and bake uncovered at 180 °C/350 °F for 10 minutes; remove and turn the veal; bake for another 10 minutes.

4 Remove the veal from the baking pan, set aside and keep warm. Remove the pork rind, leaving the cooking residues and the vegetables, add the crème fraîche, stir and put it back into the oven for a few minutes. In the meantime, untie and slice the meat. Cover with the sauce and serve.

Stuffed Shoulder of Mutton

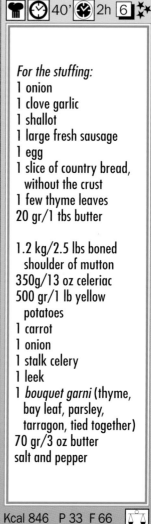

🍴 🕐 40' ⊗ 2h 6 ✿

For the stuffing:
1 onion
1 clove garlic
1 shallot
1 large fresh sausage
1 egg
1 slice of country bread,
    without the crust
1 few thyme leaves
20 gr/1 tbs butter

1.2 kg/2.5 lbs boned
    shoulder of mutton
350g/13 oz celeriac
500 gr/1 lb yellow
    potatoes
1 carrot
1 onion
1 stalk celery
1 leek
1 *bouquet garni* (thyme,
    bay leaf, parsley,
    tarragon, tied together)
70 gr/3 oz butter
salt and pepper

Kcal 846   P 33   F 66   ⚖

Fifteen minutes before starting, soak the bread in water. To prepare the stuffing, clean the onion and chop it finely; sauté it in a saucepan in melted butter; transfer to a bowl and mix with the peeled and crumbled sausage, the egg, chopped garlic, squeezed out bread and a few thyme leaves and salt and pepper. Clean the vegetables you will need to cook the meat. Butterfly the meat and place the stuffing on top; fold over and tie it together. Place the meat in a large saucepan and cover with salted water. Bring to the boil, skim and add the celery and leek cut in half, all tied together, the carrot and onion, and the *bouquet garni*. Cover and simmer for and hour and a half: cut the celeriac into chunks and add it to the pot. Peel the potatoes and cut into chunks; after 15 minutes add them to the pot as well. When the celeriac and potatoes are cooked, remove them from the pot and put them through the blender. Put this pureed mixture into a small saucepan and reduce over a high flame, mixing vigorously. When it is almost completely dry, add the butter and 5-6 tablespoons of the cooking liquid from the meat; salt and pepper to taste, and reduce slightly, stirring constantly. Degrease and strain the liquid. Remove the meat from the saucepan and slice it. Put it on a hot serving platter; serve with the sauce in a gravy boat on the side.

Pork and Vegetable Pie

First wash and clean all the vegetables, remove cores, ribs and tough leaves and parts. Chop them finely. In a bowl, mix them together with the pork, and chopped bacon add the eggs and a pinch of salt and pepper, until well blended. Grease a baking dish with lard, put the mixture into the dish and even it out. Bake at 150 °C/300 °F for 3 hours. Serve either hot or cold.

🍳 ⏱ 30' ⏲ 3h 8 ★★

250 gr/¹/₂ lb smoked streaky bacon
250 gr/¹/₂ lb lean pork
500 gr/1 lb sorrel
500 gr/1 lb spinach
1 savoy cabbage
1 bunch beet greens
3 eggs, lightly beaten
lard
salt and pepper

Kcal 518 P 20 F 40

Pheasant with Cabbage

🍖🍴 ⏱ 20'　　　⏲ 2h　　　4/5 ✹✹　　　　　Kcal 807　P 56　F 59　⚖

1 hen pheasant (or a well-ripened male), about 1.5 kg/ 3 lbs	1/2 savoy cabbage 100 gr/4 oz streaky bacon, thinly sliced	150 gr/6 oz smoked or lightly salted bacon salt and pepper

1 Pluck and dress the pheasant, then singe, wash and dry it. Cover with the slices of streaky bacon; salt and pepper the inside and set aside while you heat the oven to 220 °C/425 °F. Put the pheasant into the oven and roast about 1 and 1/2 hours.

3 Cut the bacon into strips (lardoons) gently cook it in a small saucepan with a bit of water, add the cabbage, salt and pepper to taste; cover and cook over a very low flame for 15 minutes.

2 In the meantime, clean the cabbage and scald for ten minutes in lightly salted boiling water. Drain well and cut into strips.

4 Add the bacon and cabbage to the pheasant and finish roasting. Carve the pheasant and place the pieces on a hot serving platter with the cabbage and bacon. Slightly reduce the cooking liquid and pour it over the platter.

1 pullet, 1.6-1.8 kg/3-4 lb	tarragon, thyme and parsley,	50 gr/2 oz butter
250 gr/¹/₂ lb mushrooms	tied together)	salt and pepper
1 onion	2 glasses dry white wine	
1 *bouquet garni* (bay leaves,	5 dl/1 pint crème fraîche	

The "géline de Touraine" with its black feathers is a cross between one breed of chicken that is native to the region known as "noire de Touraine" and an eastern species. The "géline", with its tender, flavorful meat is a large hen, and like many other local species of poultry it was in danger of extinction in the Fifties because of the spread of intensive breeding farms. Several years ago, however, the breeders in the Loches area resumed selective breeding of these find birds.

"Géline à la Lochoise"

1 Wash and peel the mushrooms and cut them in half (if they are very big slice them); peel and slice the onion. The pullet should already be oven-ready, that is singed, rinsed and dried. Salt and pepper the large cavity. In a large oven-proof saucepan with a lid (terracotta is best), brown it evenly in melted butter over a medium flame. After about 10 minutes, remove the bird from the pan, set it aside and keep it warm.

3 Put the pullet back into the saucepan, cover and cook in the oven at 200 °C/ 390 °F for 50 minutes; uncover for the last 10 minutes of cooking time. Remove from the oven and test with a fork for doneness.

2 Toss the mushrooms, onions and the bouquet garni into the remaining butter in the saucepan (if necessary, add a little broth). Add salt and pepper and cook over a lively flame for 5-6 minutes, pour on the wine and simmer for 5 more minutes.

4 If it is ready, put it on a platter with the onions and mushrooms. Cut the bird into pieces. Put the cooking liquid through a fine strainer and remove the *bouquet garni*. Put the strained liquid back into the saucepan, add the cream and salt and pepper to taste. Heat the sauce, being careful not to let it boil. Put the pullet back into the pan and turn the pieces gently to coat them with the sauce. Serve immediately in the pan.

Rabbit Stew with Herbs

 20' 1h,30 4 ★★

1 rabbit 1.2 kg/2.5 lbs
  (with the liver)
150 gr/6 oz streaky
  bacon (1 piece)
3-4 shallots, chopped
1 dl/³/₈ cup
  crème fraîche
1 bay leaf
1 sprig thyme
prepared mustard
3 dl/1 ¹/₂ cups chicken
  or vegetable broth
30 gr/1 oz flour
1 shot glass of cognac
  (or kirsch)
50 gr/2 oz butter
salt and pepper

Kcal 946   P 36   F 63

Cut the rabbit into pieces and dredge lightly in flour. Melt half the butter in a saucepan and brown the pieces slowly. After 5-6 minutes add the shallots, hot broth, bay leaf, thyme and salt and pepper. Stir, cover and simmer over a very low flame for 1 hour. Rinse and clean the liver, chop it coarsely and sauté it for 5-6 minutes in a skillet with the rest of the butter and the streaky bacon cut into strips. Add it to the saucepan with the rabbit and continue cooking for another 15 minutes. Remove the rabbit from the pan and put it on a hot serving platter. Remove the herbs from the pan and add the cognac; deglaze the cooking residues over a medium flame and blend in the mustard and crème fraîche, stirring gently. The ideal side dish? How about mushrooms sautéed in garlic or the famous green lentils from Berry!

Veal Roulades

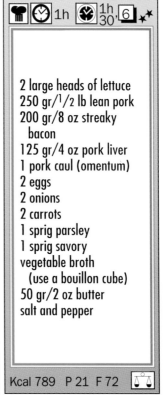

Soak the pork caul in lukewarm water and put large pot with 3.5 l/1 gallon of water on to boil. While you are waiting, clean the lettuce and discard the tough outer leaves. When the water boils, scald them for 3 minutes. Drain and rinse under cold running water. Set aside 12 pretty leaves and put the rest through the blender. Finely chop the meat, streaky bacon and liver. Put the meat mixture into a bowl and add the pureed lettuce, parsley, savory, beaten eggs and salt and pepper. Make six patties and wrap each one in two lettuce leaves. Wrap each roulade with a piece of caul cut to size. Butter an oven dish, and cover it with sliced onions and carrots and a few pats of butter. Place the roulades in the pan, douse with broth and bake at 160 °C/ 310 °F for 1 1/2 hours, basting now and then with broth so that it does not dry out too much. At the halfway point, cover the dish with aluminum foil. Serve hot.

1h · 1h 30' · 6 · ★★

2 large heads of lettuce
250 gr/^{1}/$_2$ lb lean pork
200 gr/8 oz streaky
   bacon
125 gr/4 oz pork liver
1 pork caul (omentum)
2 eggs
2 onions
2 carrots
1 sprig parsley
1 sprig savory
vegetable broth
   (use a bouillon cube)
50 gr/2 oz butter
salt and pepper

Kcal 789   P 21   F 72

Easter Meat Pie

To prepare the dough, put the flour in a mixing bowl and make a well; put the butter, in pats, into the middle along with a beaten egg and a pinch of salt. Mix at low speed, adding a drop or two of cold water if necessary, until the dough is smooth and free of lumps. Shape it into a ball, cove with a clean cloth and se aside to rest for at least hour.

1 Hard boil and shell 4 eggs (10 minutes). Preheat the oven to 220 °C/ 425 °F. Coarsely chop the veal, the smoked and streaky bacon, with the parsley, onion and shallots. Place the mixture into a bowl and add the peeled and crumbled sausages, two eggs, the thyme and broken bay leaf; add salt and pepper in moderation because the pork is already salty.

2 Roll out the dough to a thickness of 3 mm (1/4 inch) and make two rectangles: one twice the size of the other. Save the scraps for trim later. Place the larger of the two rectangles on a baking pan cov-

ered with buttered aluminum foil or over paper. Place half the meat mixture on top leaving 3-4 cm (1 1/2 inches along the edges. Place the hard boiled eggs end-to end along the middle and cover with the rest of the filling.

3 Moisten the edges of the dough with a wet pastry brush and fold them inwards. Cover with the smaller piece of dough and press down the edges to seal. Decorate the top with the dough scraps. Make a tube out of oven paper and put it in the middle of the dough, it will serve as a chimney to let the steam out while baking. Brush the surface with beaten egg yolk. Place in the oven and lower the temperature to 180 °C/350 °F and bake for 1 hour. If the top browns too quickly, when half done, cover with a piece of aluminum foil. Remove the tube, and serve the pie with green salad on the side.

🍳 ⏱ 45'+1h	⏲ 1h	🔢 8 ★★	Kcal 864 P 29 F 65	⚖

For the dough:
350 gr/13 oz flour (plus some
　more for your work table)
170 gr/7 oz butter
1 egg
salt

For the filling:
400 gr/1 lb roast leg of veal
150 gr/6 oz bacon,
　not smoked, in 1 piece
100 gr/4 oz streaky bacon,
　in 1 piece
2 fresh sausages

6 eggs plus 1 yolk
1 onion
3-4 shallots
1 bay leaf
1 sprig parsley, 1 sprig thyme
20 gr/ 1 oz butter
salt and pepper

| 🍗🕐 30' | 🕐 45' | 6 ⋆⋆ | Kcal 933 P 46 F 69 | ⚖ |

1 pullet, 1.6-1.8 kg/3-4 lb	250 gr/^{1}/$_2$ lb mushrooms	^{1}/$_2$ l/2 cups chicken broth
1 onion	3 dl/1 ^{1}/$_2$ cups crème fraîche	2 glasses red wine
1-2 cloves garlic	1 egg yolk	60 gr/2 oz butter
2 shallots	the juice of 1 lemon	salt and pepper
1 ripe tomato	30 g/1 oz flour	

Pullet with Mushrooms and Wine Sauce

1 Wash and peel the mushrooms and all the vegetables. The pullet should be singed, rinsed and dried, and cut into 10 pieces. Dredge the pieces in flour. Melt the butter in a skillet and brown the pullet, season with salt and pepper, cover and cook over a low flame for 40 minutes, turning the pieces so they do not stick. (If necessary add a tablespoon or two of broth). Remove the pullet from the skillet and arrange the pieces on a serving platter and keep warm.

3 Sauté the mushrooms with a pat of butter in a saucepan, add the rest of the broth, cover and simmer for 20 minutes. Put the mushrooms into the skillet, add the crème fraîche and stir to blend; salt and pepper to taste. Without letting it boil, add the pieces of pullet, and turn gently in the sauce. When they are nice and hot, remove the skillet from the stove and put the meat back on the serving platter.

2 Pour the wine into the skillet, bring it to a boil over a high flame and deglaze the cooking residues. Add the tomato, cut into pieces, and the finely chopped onion and shallots. Add half the broth, cover the skillet, lower the flame and cook slowly until the liquid is reduced by half.

4 Beat the egg with lemon juice and add it to the creamy cooking residues in the skillet, and then pour it over the meat. Serve immediately with white rice on the side.

Chicken with Mushrooms

Singe, rinse and dry the chicken; then cut it into 10-12 pieces. Salt it moderately. Melt the fat in a saucepan and brown the chicken evenly. Remove the pieces, put them on a tray and keep warm. Using the fat in the saucepan (replace it if has blackened) slowly sauté the garlic, then add the parsley, the chicken, a dash of ground nutmeg and stir. Cover and simmer for 30 minutes. In the meantime, clean the mushrooms, break them up and season with a little salt and pepper; sauté gently for about fifteen minutes in a skillet with melted fat. Five minutes before the chicken is ready, add the mushrooms to the saucepan along with the shot glass of eau de vie; stir gently and serve immediately.

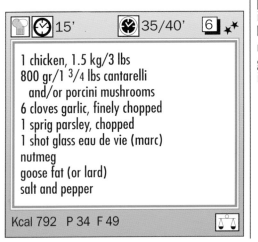

15' 35/40' 6

1 chicken, 1.5 kg/3 lbs
800 gr/1 3/4 lbs cantarelli and/or porcini mushrooms
6 cloves garlic, finely chopped
1 sprig parsley, chopped
1 shot glass eau de vie (marc)
nutmeg
goose fat (or lard)
salt and pepper

Kcal 792 P 34 F 49

"Rillons"

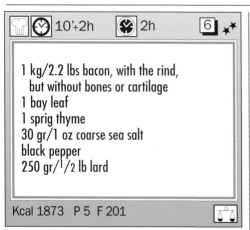

🎩 ⏰ 10'+2h ❀ 2h 6 ⋆⋆

1 kg/2.2 lbs bacon, with the rind,
   but without bones or cartilage
1 bay leaf
1 sprig thyme
30 gr/1 oz coarse sea salt
black pepper
250 gr/¹/₂ lb lard

Kcal 1873 P 5 F 201

Cut the bacon into evenly sized bits without removing the rind; if necessary singe and rinse to remove any bristles. Prepare a bowl with the salt, freshly ground pepper and the herbs; add the bacon bits and stir until they are evenly coated. Set aside to rest for a few hours. Slowly heat the lard in a large saucepan being careful so that it does not get smoky. Add the bacon bits and brown slowly in the melted lard. Cover the pan, lower the flame as far as you can and simmer for a couple of hours until the meat is very tender. Every now and then check to see if you should add a little hot water, and stir gently. The *rillons* can be served as a dish – drain well on paper towels – or refrigerated for a couple of weeks. To store, put in glass jars with the cooking grease and add a layer of lard to cover; cover the top with paper.

Some people marinate the bacon overnight in white wine (Vouvray is the best) with a carrot, bits of shallot, bay leaf and thyme, and then cook it with the marinade herbs in a cheesecloth bag.

Braised Eel with Prunes

1 An hour before you start, soak the prunes in a glass of the wine you will use for cooking. If you are using fresh plums, cut them in half, and remove the pits, but keep the skins. Wash and peel the mushrooms, slice them – and the onion. If the eels are small, you need not skin them, just cut off the heads and gut them. Cut them into 4 cm (2 inch) long pieces and dredge lightly in flour. Brown them evenly in a skillet in ¹/₂ of the butter, drain and set aside.

3 Add the eel, salt and pepper to taste, add the prunes and the *bouquet garni*, and pour on enough wine to cover. Put on the lid and simmer over a very low flame for 1 hour, remove the lid for last 10 minutes of cooking time. Put the eel and onions onto a serving platter and keep warm.

4 Deglaze the cooking residues over a low flame with the rest of the butter and a tablespoon of flour, then serve the eel with this sauce.

One variation says you can add 120g/5 oz bacon bits, or smoked bacon to the onions and mushrooms.

2 Using the same skillet – and butter, adding more if necessary – sauté the mushrooms, onion and shallot.

20'+1h 1h20' 4/6 Kcal 852 P 38 F 57

1 kg/2.2 lbs medium sized eels
20 prunes
10 green onions
1 bottle red wine

250 gr/½ lb mushrooms
1 *bouquet garni* (bay leaves, parsley and thyme, tied into a bunch)
1 shallot, finely chopped

40 gr/2 tablespoons flour
100 gr/4 oz butter
salt and pepper

Oven-baked Frogs' Legs and Eel

🍳 ⏰ 1h ⏱ 30' 4/6 ★★

1 kg/2.2 lbs medium size
  eels, cleaned,
  decapitated and skinned
2 dozen frogs' legs
2 large artichokes
1 clove garlic
1 sprig parsley
1 lemon
1/2 glass dry white wine
120 gr/5 oz butter
salt and pepper

Kcal 836   P 41   F 65

Scald the unpeeled garlic in a glass of water for 10 minutes; use another saucepan with a glass of water to scald the parsley for just 1 minute. Drain the garlic, peel it and put it through the blender with the parsley and 30 gr/ 1 oz softened butter. Set aside. Clean the artichokes remove the leaves and the choke to get the "hearts." Put the hearts in a bowl filled with water and lemon juice (this will prevent them from turning black). Pat dry and cut into 8 sections and sauté in 20 gr/1 tbs butter, adding 1/2 glass of wine and a pinch of salt. Cut the eel into 6 cm (2-3 inch) long pieces and put them on a baking sheet that is covered with aluminum foil or oven paper along with the frogs' legs. Melt 40 gr /2 oz butter and brush the eel and frogs legs. Bake at 200 °C/390 °F for 10 minutes.

In the meantime, melt the garlic and parsley butter in a saucepan; add a ladle of water, the rest of the butter in pats and beat with a wire whisk. Salt and pepper to taste, remove from the stove and distribute the sauce on individual plates, along with the frogs' legs, eel and artichoke hearts.

Frogs' Legs in Wine Sauce

Dredge the frogs' legs in flour, and shake to remove any excess. Melt $1/2$ of the butter in a skillet and brown the frogs legs slowly. Add salt and pepper and then the shallots and parsley, pour on the wine and let it evaporate partly. Remove the frogs' legs from the skillet, drain and arrange them on a serving platter and set aside keeping them warm. Reduce the sauce in the skillet by half, add the cream, and slowly add the beaten egg yolks and the rest of the butter. Complete the sauce by adding a few drops of lemon juice, pour over the frogs' legs and serve immediately.

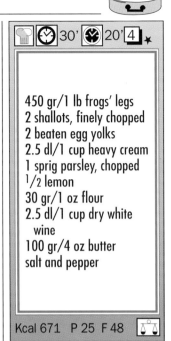

30' 20' 4 ★

450 gr/1 lb frogs' legs
2 shallots, finely chopped
2 beaten egg yolks
2.5 dl/1 cup heavy cream
1 sprig parsley, chopped
$1/2$ lemon
30 gr/1 oz flour
2.5 dl/1 cup dry white wine
100 gr/4 oz butter
salt and pepper

Kcal 671 P 25 F 48

Baked Stuffed Carp

Before you begin, soak the bread in the milk for 15 minutes. Remove the scales from the carp, gut it and wash it thoroughly inside and out. Peel the onion and carrot and slice into disks.

Line the bottom of a suitably sized oven pan with the slices of streaky bacon and arrange the carrot and onion slices evenly on top.

Finely chop the ham, parsley, onion and garlic together. In a mixing bowl, add the two egg yolks, the squeezed out bread and a pinch of salt and pepper to the ham mixture.

Stuff the carp and sew it closed without pulling too tightly.

Place the fish on the bed of carrots and onion and cover with the rest of the streaky bacon, put the remaining carrot and onion slices on top, along with a shredded bay leaf, the tips of a sprig of parsley and of thyme. Moisten with a glass of wine and a tablespoon of vinegar.

Bake in a preheated oven at 200 °C/390 °F for about 40 minutes. Put the cooking liquid through a fine strainer and pour it over the carp and vegetables just before serving.

The city of Blois with the gothic church of St. Nicolas and the castle.

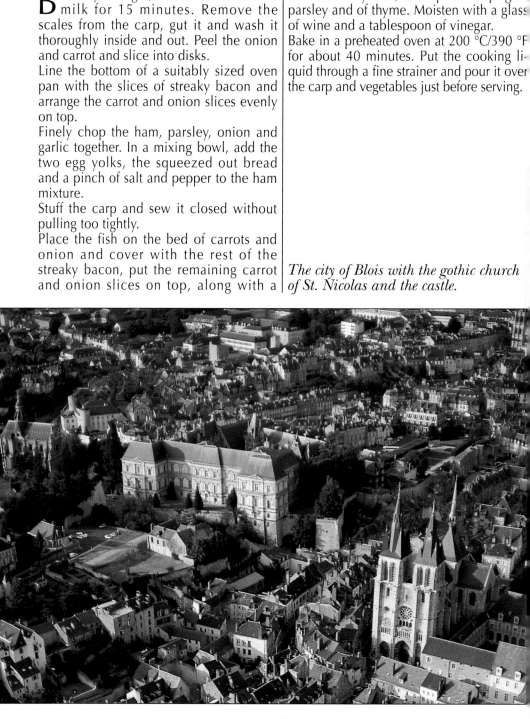

🍳 20'+15'	⏱ 45'	4 ★★	Kcal 630 P 16 F 45	⚖

1 carp,
   about 1/1.5 kg/ 2-3 lbs
120 gr/5 oz streaky bacon,
   thinly sliced
1 onion
1 carrot
1 tablespoon vinegar
1 glass dry white wine

1 bay leaf
1 sprig parsley
1 sprig thyme

For the stuffing:
2 slices ham (or 100 gr/4 oz
   finely chopped leftover
   cooked white meat)

1 onion, 1 clove garlic
1 sprig parsley
2 egg yolks (one raw, one
   hardboiled)
1 slice white bread, without the
   crust
1/2 glass milk
salt and pepper

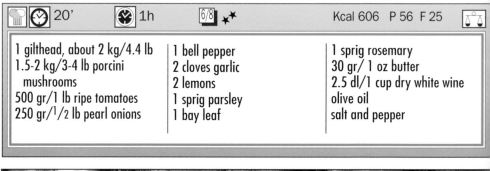

🍳⏱ 20'	🌸 1h	6/8 ✦★	Kcal 606 P 56 F 25	⚖

1 gilthead, about 2 kg/4.4 lb 1.5-2 kg/3-4 lb porcini mushrooms 500 gr/1 lb ripe tomatoes 250 gr/$^1/_2$ lb pearl onions	1 bell pepper 2 cloves garlic 2 lemons 1 sprig parsley 1 bay leaf	1 sprig rosemary 30 gr/ 1 oz butter 2.5 dl/1 cup dry white wine olive oil salt and pepper

Gilthead with Mushrooms

1 Remove the scales from the fish, gut it and then rinse it and dry it. Season the cavity with a pinch of salt and pepper, bay leaf and rosemary. Peel the onions; clean the pepper, remove the seeds and white membrane and cut it into triangular pieces. Slice the tomatoes, remove the seeds; wash and slice the lemons. Place the gilthead in a large oven dish, pour 2 tablespoons olive oil over it and then cover the fish with lemon slices and pepper triangles. Pour the wine over it and then arrange the tomatoes and onions in the dish, add salt and pepper and bake at 200 °C/390 °F for 1 hour.

2 In the meantime, clean the mushrooms – scrape off any dirt and dust. If they are big, cut them into chunks. Melt the butter in a skillet with 3-4 tablespoons olive oil and sauté the mushrooms over a lively flame. Sprinkle with finely chopped garlic and parsley. Stir and season with a pinch of salt and pepper; lower the flame and cook slowly for about 20 minutes. When the fish is done, surround it with the mushrooms and serve immediately.

The kitchen in the Château de La Ferté - St.-Aubin.

Salmon with Sorrel

The day before you actually cook, clean the sorrel and scald it in boiling salted water; put it in a strainer to drain and dry overnight. The next day arrange the onion slices in a baking dish, put the fish filets on top with lemon slices all around; season with salt and pepper, pour on enough wine to cover the fish halfway and bake at 180 °C/350 °F for 20 minutes. In the meantime, finely chop the sorrel. Melt the butter along with 2 tablespoons cream in a saucepan, add the sorrel, stir, add salt and pepper and cook slowly for 10 minutes. Then prepare the sauce, a sort of *beurre blanc.* In a saucepan, combine the shallots, 1 glass wine and _ glass vinegar. Cook over a very low flame until the liquid has evaporated, add the cream and quickly bring to the boil. Lower the flame blend in the rest of the butter while stirring constantly with a whisk. Salt to taste, arrange the sorrel puree all around the fish and pour the sauce over it all.

30' +10h 20' 6 ★★

1 kg/2.2 lbs salmon filets
(or pike or pikeperch)
1.5 kg/3 lbs of bunches
of sorrel
1 large onion, sliced
1 lemon, sliced
3 dl/1 ^{1}/2 cups dry white
wine
cream
40 gr/2 oz butter
salt and pepper

For the sauce:
4 shallots, finely chopped
1 glass dry white wine
^{1}/2 glass white wine
vinegar
1 dl/^{3}/8 cup cream
100 gr/4 oz butter
salt and pepper

Kcal 1636   P 52   F 65

Loire Valley Fish Soup

🗑️ 🕐 20' ⏱️ 45' 6 ⭐

Scale the fish; if the eel is large, remove the skin; gut and cut into pieces. In a saucepan combine about 2 liters/2 quarts cold water, the wine, a inch of salt, peppercorns and the *bouquet garni*. Bring to the boil, lower the flame and add the fish pieces; simmer for about 2 minutes.

In the meantime, peel the potatoes, clean and slice the leek and onion. Melt the butter in a saucepan and gently sauté the leek and onion, with the lid on so they stay white. Drain the fish. Put the cooking liquid through a sieve and save it. Put the fish into the saucepan with the leek and onion, cover with sliced potatoes. Add the fish broth, if it is not enough to cover the potatoes add a little hot water. Salt and pepper to taste. Bring to the boil and then simmer over a medium flame until the potatoes are cooked. Serve the fish over slices of toasted bread, cover with the potatoes and garnish with aromatic herbs.

1.5 kg/3 lbs mixed
    fresh water fish
    (carp, perch, eel, pike,
    tench, chub, etc.)
4 medium yellow
    potatoes (bintje)
1 leek
1 onion
1 *bouquet garni*
    (tarragon, parsley and
    thyme, all tied together)
1/2 l/2 cups dry
    white wine
slices of toasted country
    bread (for serving)
30 gr/1 oz butter
salt and peppercorns

Kcal 1845   P 38   F 19 ⚖️

Beet Greens au Gratin

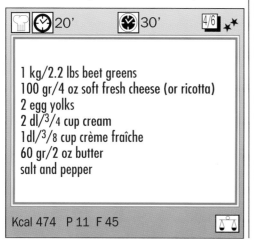

⏱ 20' ⏲ 30' 4/6 ★★

1 kg/2.2 lbs beet greens
100 gr/4 oz soft fresh cheese (or ricotta)
2 egg yolks
2 dl/³/₄ cup cream
1dl/³/₈ cup crème fraîche
60 gr/2 oz butter
salt and pepper

Kcal 474   P 11   F 45

Wash the beet greens and discard the tough stems, cut the leaves into 2x4 cm (1x2 inch) pieces. In a saucepan melt 30 gr/1 oz butter add the beet greens, cover and cook over a low flame for 15 minutes. Add the cream and cook for another 5 minutes.

In the meantime, melt the cheese in another saucepan over a very low flame, then add it to the beet greens.

Remove the saucepan from the stove and let it cool to lukewarm. In a mixing bowl, combine the egg yolks and crème fraîche, add salt and pepper and then blend this into the beet greens.

Pour the mixture into a buttered oven dish and bake at 220 °C/425 °F for about 10 minutes.

Stewed Mushrooms and Onions

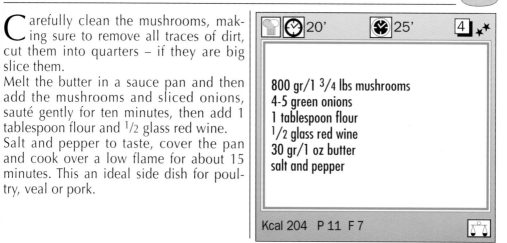

Carefully clean the mushrooms, making sure to remove all traces of dirt, cut them into quarters – if they are big slice them.

Melt the butter in a sauce pan and then add the mushrooms and sliced onions, sauté gently for ten minutes, then add 1 tablespoon flour and $^{1}/_{2}$ glass red wine.

Salt and pepper to taste, cover the pan and cook over a low flame for about 15 minutes. This an ideal side dish for poultry, veal or pork.

🍳⏲ 20'   ❀ 25'   4 ✶✶

800 gr/1 $^{3}/_{4}$ lbs mushrooms
4-5 green onions
1 tablespoon flour
$^{1}/_{2}$ glass red wine
30 gr/1 oz butter
salt and pepper

Kcal 204   P 11   F 7

Stewed Green Onions in Butter Sauce ▶

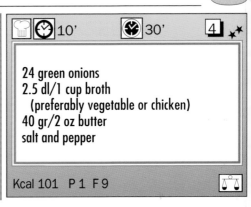

Carefully clean the onions. Heat the broth in a saucepan, add the butter and stir gently until it melts. Salt and pepper to taste, then add the onions, cover and cook for 30 minutes over a very low flame, stirring now and then. If there is too much liquid, uncover the pan after about 15 minutes.

Serve the onions on a platter with the thick sauce. This is a perfect accompaniment to pork or lamb and mutton.

If you like, you can serve the onions as a main course over slices of toasted country bread.

🍳⏱ 10'   ✺ 30'   4 ⋆★

24 green onions
2.5 dl/1 cup broth
    (preferably vegetable or chicken)
40 gr/2 oz butter
salt and pepper

Kcal 101 P 1 F 9

The picturesque kitchen in the Château de Montreuil-Bellay.

Fresh Peas with Tomatoes

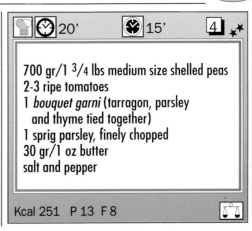

Wash the tomatoes, cut them in half, remove the seeds and then cut them into chunks. Melt the butter in a saucepan, add the tomatoes and let them soften over a low flame for 3-4 minutes. Add the washed, drained peas, the *bouquet garni* and a pinch of salt and pepper. Cover the pan and simmer for about 12 minutes. Remove the bouquet garni, sprinkle the peas with the chopped parsley and serve.

🍳⏱ 20'   ✺ 15'   4 ⋆★

700 gr/1 3/4 lbs medium size shelled peas
2-3 ripe tomatoes
1 *bouquet garni* (tarragon, parsley
    and thyme tied together)
1 sprig parsley, finely chopped
30 gr/1 oz butter
salt and pepper

Kcal 251 P 13 F 8

| 🍲🕐 20'+30' | ❄ 45' | 4/6 ★★ | | Kcal 537 P 13 F 32 | ⚖ |

900g-1 kg/2 lbs yellow potatoes (bintje)	1 bay leaf	1 dl/³/₈ cup milk
1 shallot, finely chopped	1 sprig tarragon	50 gr/2 oz butter
60 gr/2 oz gruyere cheese, grated in flakes	1 sprig chives	salt and pepper
	1 sprig thyme	
	2 dl/³/₄ cup crème fraîche	

Oven-baked Potatoes with Cheese

1 Clean the herbs. Slowly heat the milk in a saucepan and add the herbs; simmer for 10 minutes and then put the mixture through a sieve so the milk pours into a large bowl.

3 Butter a baking dish and arrange the potato slices on the bottom of the dish, season with salt and pepper. Pour on a little cream, keep on making layers and end with a layer of cream, sprinkle with fresh, chopped thyme. Cover with aluminum foil and bake for just 30 minutes.

2 Wash and peel the potatoes, slice them into disks (3-4 mm/ $^1/_2$ inch thick). Put them into the bowl with the milk and the chopped shallot and soak for 30 minutes. Preheat your oven to 180 °C/350 °F.

4 Remove the dish from the oven, uncover and sprinkle with the flaked cheese; bake for 15 minutes more, garnish with snipped chervil or chives and then serve immediately. This is a wonderful side dish for mutton and rabbit.

Baked Apple Dumplings

1 To prepare the dough, put the flour into a large mixing bowl and make a well in the middle. Put the butter, in pats into the well along with the sugar and a pinch of salt. Blend gently using your hands or the mixer on low speed; stop mixing every now and then so that the mixture does not get hot. Keep working until it is smooth with no lumps. Cover with a clean cloth and set aside for 1 hour.

3 Roll out the dough to a thickness of 3 mm (1/4 inch) and make discs that are big enough to cover the apples (the diameter should be double that of the apples') Put an apple in the middle of each disc, wrap it in the dough and pull up the edges. Close the "bundle" by pressing the dough firmly with your fingers at the "north pole" of the apples.

2 Pare and core the apples. Close the bottom with a pat of butter and fill the cavity with sugar.

4 Beat the egg yolk together with the milk and brush the upper half of each apple bundle with this mixture. Line an oven dish with buttered aluminum foil or oven paper and bake at 200 °C/ 390 °F for 30 minutes. Keep an eye on them, if they start to get too brown lower the temperature to 180 °C/350 °F.

6 medium rennet
  or Granny Smith apples
150 gr/6 oz butter
150 gr/6 oz sugar
1 egg yolk

1.5 dl/¹/₂ cup milk

For the dough:
300 gr/12 oz flour
200 gr/8 oz butter

40 gr/2 oz sugar
salt

500 gr/1 lb flour
250 gr/¹/₂ lb sugar
1 egg and 1 yolk

1 tablespoon rum
2 tablespoons black coffee
250 gr/¹/₂ lb butter

salt

"Broyé"

1 Pour the sugar – with a pinch of salt – into a large mixing bowl. Make a well in the middle and cut in the butter. Mix gently by hand.

3 Put the dough into a cake pan and level it out to a thickness of 1 cm (1/2 inch). Use the tines of a fork to scratch a pattern into it.

2 Add the flour, one tablespoon at a time as you knead to get a smooth dough, blend in 1 tablespoon rum. Continue kneading until the dough separates from the sides of the bowl.

4 Beat the egg yolk with the coffee and brush it over the dough. Bake at 180 °C/ 350 °F for 30 minutes. Remove from the oven and cool thoroughly before removing it from the pan. This is a fine dessert with sweet wines and it is great for breakfast with coffee or tea.

The secret to making a perfect Broyé is in the long, hand kneading.

Chilled Berry Pudding

Beat the egg whites to soft peaks with a pinch of salt and set aside.
Whip the cream, blend in the sugar and the egg whites.
Line individual cups with enough oven paper or foil so that you can fold it up to cover the surface; put some of the mixture in each cup and refrigerate for 8 hours.
Remove and turn out onto serving dishes and serve with fresh berries (or even raspberry sauce).

15'+8h   6

5 dl/1 pint whipping cream
4 egg whites
100 gr/4 oz sugar
berries (for serving)
salt

Kcal 398 P 6 F 31

Almond Cake

Preheat the oven to 180 °C/ 350 °F. Put the almonds through the blender to get a powder, not a paste. Soften 250 gr/1/2 lb butter and blend in the sugar and almonds. Gradually add the eggs, flour and 1 shot glass of rum.

Butter a cake pan and pour in the mixture, smooth the top, and bake at 180 °C/350 °F for 45 minutes. When the cake is done, remove it from the oven and pour on another shot glass of rum.

Let the cake cool complete and spread the top with 2-3 tablespoon apricot jam diluted with a little hot water.

In a mixing bowl, dilute enough confectioner's sugar in the last glass of rum to make a glaze that you will spread over the top of the cake. This cake is best, if you serve it a couple of days after you make it.

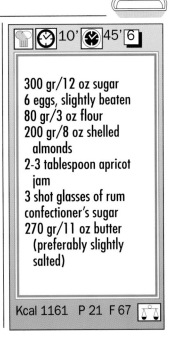

🍴 ⏲ 10' ⏱ 45' 6

300 gr/12 oz sugar
6 eggs, slightly beaten
80 gr/3 oz flour
200 gr/8 oz shelled
   almonds
2-3 tablespoon apricot
   jam
3 shot glasses of rum
confectioner's sugar
270 gr/11 oz butter
   (preferably slightly
   salted)

Kcal 1161   P 21   F 67 ⚖

"Poirat"

1 Prepare the dough ahead of time, by combining the flour, softened butter, egg yolk, vanilla-flavored sugar and a pinch of salt; set aside for 2 hours. Peel, core and slice the pears. Put the slices into a bowl, moisten with the liquor and dust with the sugar mixed with a good sprinkling of freshly ground pepper. Set aside for 1 hour.

3 Make a hole in the middle; shape a cylinder out of aluminum foil or oven paper and put in the hole, this will act a a chimney to let the steam escape. Brush the surface of the dough with beaten egg yolk and bake at 220°C/425 °F for 3! minutes, then lower the temperature to 180 °C/350 °F and bake 20 minute: longer.

2 Roll out the dough into a 5mm (1/2 inch) thick circle. Drain the pears, keep the liquid. Put the pears in the middle of the dough and fold the edges towards the middle to cover the pears and seal by pressing with your fingers.

4 Dilute the cream with a few tablespoon of the liquid so that it flows evenly. Tilt the cake slightly and gradually pour the liquid into the middle of the "smokestack."

| 🍳⏱ 40'+2h | 🕐 1h | 6 | Kcal 828 P 9 F 31 | ⚖ |

For the dough:
300 gr/12 oz flour
150 gr/6 oz butter
1 egg yolk
30 gr/1 oz vanilla-flavored sugar

salt

700 gr/1 3/4 lbs Williams pears
1 dl/³/₈ cup heavy cream

1 dl/³/₈ cup Williams pear liqueur
1 egg
freshly ground black pepper
60 gr/2 oz sugar

Spicy Apple Tart

1 Prepare the sauce. Peel the lemon and squeeze the juice into a saucepan: add the apple juice, lemon peel, 1 tablespoon honey and the butter. Bring to the boil and cook for 2 minutes. Remove the pan from the stove and blend in 1/2 teaspoon of the spices.

3 Put the dish on the stove over a low flame and cook until the sugar and butter are a nice even golden color; bake at 180 °C/350 °F for 40 minutes. In the meantime, roll the pastry into a circle (25 cm/9 inches) in diameter.

2 Peel the apples and cut them in quarters. Butter the bottom of a baking dish (about 16 cm/7 inches in diameter, 5 cm/2 inch high sides), sprinkle with sugar and put the apples on top so they sink into the butter.

4 Remove the pan from the oven, cover the apples with the pastry dough and bake for ten minutes more, until the top is golden. Cool to lukewarm and then turn out onto a round platter so that the apples are on top. Drench with the sauce and serve.

1 kg/2.2 lbs rennet apples	*For the spice sauce:*	50 gr/2 oz butter
125 gr/4 oz butter, softened	1 lemon	ground cinnamon, liquorice
75 gr/3 oz sugar	2.5 dl/1 cup apple juice	and nutmeg
100 gr/4 oz puff pastry	1 tablespoon acacia honey	

Table of Contents

THE CUISINE OF THE KINGS

Project and editorial concept: Casa Editrice Bonechi
Series Editor: Alberto Andreini
Editor: Paolo Piazzesi
Graphics and cover: Maria Rosanna Malagrinò
Layout: Marina Miele
Edited by: Rina Bucci
English Translation by: Julia Weiss Goldin

All the recipes in this book have been tested by our team of chefs.
In the kitchen: Lisa Mugnai
Nutritionist: Dr. John Luke Hili

The photographs of the foods, property of the Bonechi Archives, were taken by Andrea Fantauzzo.

The photographs of the settings, property of the Bonechi Archives, were taken by:
Gianni Dagli Orti, Paolo Giambone, Andrea Pistolesi.

© by CASA EDITRICE BONECHI, Florence – Italy
e-mail: bonechi@bonechi.it   website: www.bonechi.it

Printed in Italy by Centro Stampa Editoriale Bonechi.

***